KITCHEN CHEMISTRY

A FOOD SCIENCE COOKBOOK

by
Andrea
Debbink

illustrated
by Emily
Balsley

Published by American Girl Publishing

No part of this book may be used or reproduced in any manner whatsoever without written permission except in the case of brief quotations embodied in critical articles and reviews.

21 22 23 24 25 26 27 QP 10 9 8 7 6 5 4 3 2 1

Editorial Development: Andrea Debbink
Art Direction and Design: Gretchen Becker
Illustrations: Emily Balsley
Photos: Chris Hynes Photography
Food Styling: Stef Endres, Laura DeVries
Production: Caryl Boyer, Cynthia Stiles, Jodi Knueppel

Cataloging-in-Publication Data available from the Library of Congress

americangirl.com/service

DEAR READER,

Cooking is part of everyday life. You likely eat a lot of food that's prepared for you by other people: parents, school cafeteria staff, restaurant chefs. But you're also at an age when you're experimenting in the kitchen yourself. You might help cook meals for family and friends. Or you might cook just because it's fun!

People enjoy cooking for many reasons. Cooking can be an art. Frosting a cupcake, tossing a colorful salad, braiding bread dough—these are all skills that make food taste and look delicious. You can think of frosting as paint. Or see a perfectly layered sandwich as sculpture.

But cooking is not only an art; it's also a science. Food science is a subject you can study in college. But you don't have to wait until then. You can start learning the science of cooking right now in your own kitchen. The type of science that's most helpful for cooking is chemistry. Chemistry is the study of what things are made of (called *matter*) and how matter behaves. When you understand chemistry, you can understand how ingredients and cooking methods work.

Chemistry helps solve the mysteries of the kitchen: why bread dough rises when baked (page 59), how grilled sandwiches turn crispy and golden brown (page 82), and how creamy hummus can be made from a can of chickpeas (page 57). These science secrets can help you become a better chef. Are crispy cookies your favorite? There's an ingredient that makes them crispy. Do you have a parent who doesn't eat gluten? There are ways to make bread without it! Or do you want a tastier breakfast smoothie? Science can help with that, too. The kitchen is your lab and every recipe is a new chance to experiment. Let's get started!

YOUR FRIENDS at AMERICAN GIRL

Contents

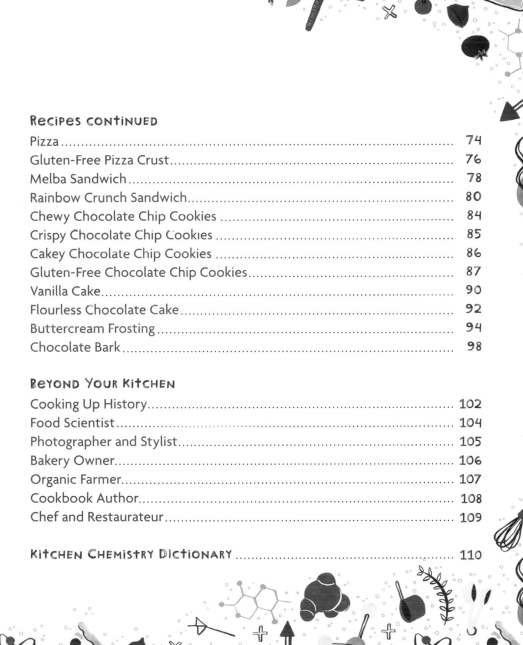

Recipes continued

Beyond Your Kitchen

Kitchen Chemistry Dictionary

How to Use This Book

Look for these icons to learn the science behind a recipe!

The recipe name

FOOD SCIENCE

KITCHEN CHEMISTRY Les

EGGSHELL

EGG WHITE

AIR CELL

SCRAMBLED EGGS

What you'll need

🖐 Ask an adult to help you with this reci

INGREDIENTS
• 2 eggs
• 1 tablespoon milk
• ¼ teaspoon salt
• ¼ teaspoon pepper
• Nonstick cooking spray

PROTEINS
EVAPORATION
COAGULATION

DIRECTIONS
1. Crack the eggs into a small mixing bowl. Whisk the eggs until the yolks and whites are blended together, about 1 minute.

How to make it

milk, salt, and pepper, and whisk

small frying pan with nonstick ng spray. Place the pan on a burner, and ask an adult to turn the burner to low heat. Let the pan warm up for about 2 minutes.

4. Slowly pour the egg mixture into the pan. Use a plastic or wooden spatula to push the eggs around in the pan every 30 seconds or so. As soon as the egg mixture becomes solid, turn off the burner. Use a spatula to transfer the eggs to a plate.

Egg yolks can be pale yellow, deep orange, or any shade in between! And the shells of chicken eggs can come in many colors—even light blue or pale pink. The yolk and shell colors depend on the breed of the chicken that laid it and the type of food she ate.

EGGS are made up of water and proteins. **Protein** is a type of **nutrient** that supplies energy and helps build muscle. It helps give food its structure and texture.

When an egg is cooked, the water in the egg heats up a This is called **evaporation**; it's when a liquid changes to water makes the proteins in the egg join more tightly egg's texture. This is called **coagulation**. If you cook too much water and the texture becomes rubbery.

HEAT →

An uncooked egg has a lot of water.

Heat causes th to evapora

Any word in teal can be found in the Kitchen Chemistry Dictionary on pages 110–111.

30

6

SAFETY GUIDELINES

Follow these guidelines to keep you (and others) safe when you cook!

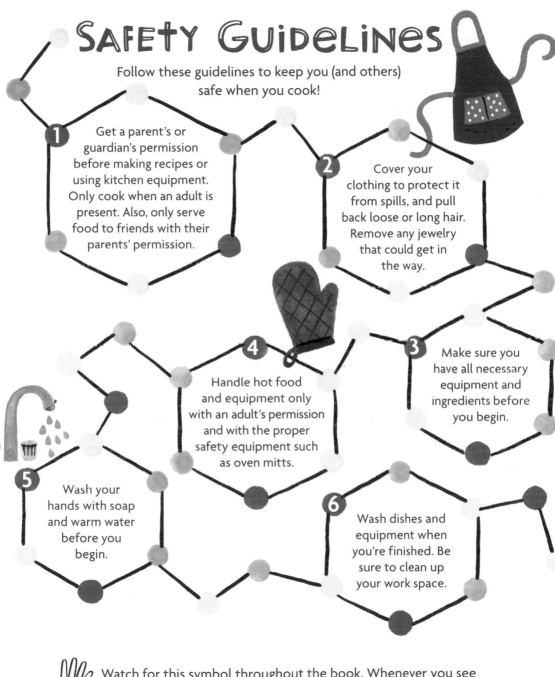

1 Get a parent's or guardian's permission before making recipes or using kitchen equipment. Only cook when an adult is present. Also, only serve food to friends with their parents' permission.

2 Cover your clothing to protect it from spills, and pull back loose or long hair. Remove any jewelry that could get in the way.

3 Make sure you have all necessary equipment and ingredients before you begin.

4 Handle hot food and equipment only with an adult's permission and with the proper safety equipment such as oven mitts.

5 Wash your hands with soap and warm water before you begin.

6 Wash dishes and equipment when you're finished. Be sure to clean up your work space.

Watch for this symbol throughout the book. Whenever you see it, be sure to ask for an adult's help with that step or recipe.

KitcHEN TooLS AND EQuiPMENt

Most of the recipes in this book use common kitchen tools and equipment. Depending on what you make, here are some of the items you'll need.

1	Mc

measuring cups

6	Fp

food processor

11	Pw

plastic wrap

12	Wp

wax paper

13	Pp

parchment paper

14	Cs

cookie sheet

19	Sp

saucepan

20	Fr

frying pan

21	Cb

cutting board

22	Pp

pizza pan

2	Ms	3	Lc	4	Mb	5	B

measuring spoons

liquid measuring cup

mixing bowl

blender

7	W	8	Sc	9	C	10	St

whisk

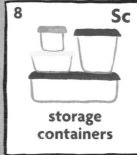
storage containers

colander

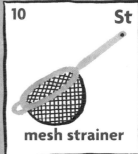
mesh strainer

15	Rs	16	S	17	Ks	18	Mj

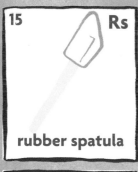
rubber spatula

spatula

kitchen scissors

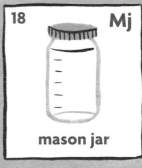
mason jar

23	Pc	24	Pm	25	Lp	26	Wr

pastry cutter

potato masher

loaf pan

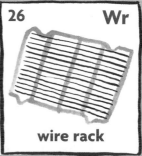
wire rack

COOKING SKILLS

Here are some skills you might use in the kitchen.
Not sure how to do something? Ask a parent or
a more experienced cook!

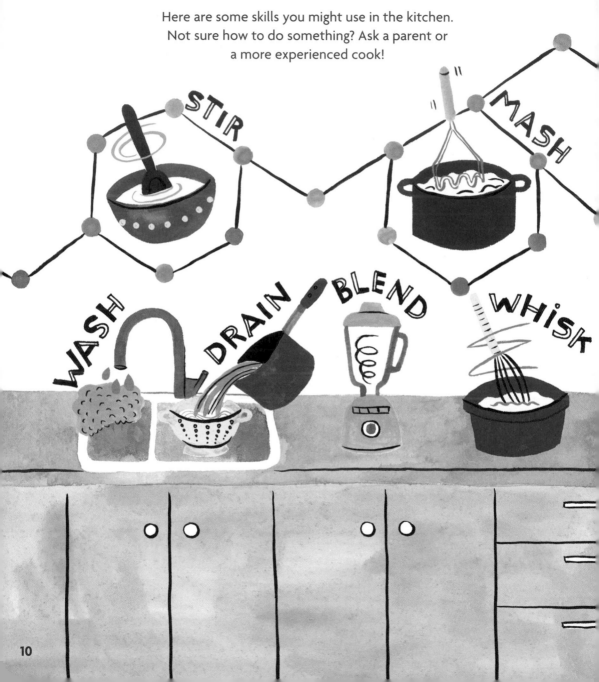

STIR

MASH

WASH

DRAIN

BLEND

WHISK

BEAT

ROLL OUT

BOIL

SIMMER

ROAST

BAKE

11

MEASURING

When you measure ingredients for a recipe, make sure you use the correct tools.

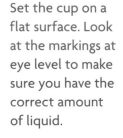

MILK

Set the cup on a flat surface. Look at the markings at eye level to make sure you have the correct amount of liquid.

For liquids, use a liquid measuring cup like this.

Fill the measuring cup or spoon until it overflows; then use the flat edge of a butter knife to scrape it across the top so it's flat and smooth.

For measuring dry ingredients, use measuring cups and spoons that look like this:

FOOD SCiENcE 101

THE SCIENCE OF FLAVOR

People usually decide whether they like or dislike a food based on three factors: taste, aroma, and texture. A food's flavor is the combination of these three qualities.

TASTE + AROMA + TEXTURE = FLAVOR

TASTE

For a long time, people thought that taste came only from our taste buds. (Taste buds are the tiny bumps all over your tongue. They're called **receptors** because they take in information from the food you eat and send messages about it to your brain.)

In the past, scientists thought the tongue could detect four tastes—sweet, sour, bitter, and salty—and was divided into different sections like this: ➔

In 2002, after almost 100 years of debate (no, really!), scientists officially recognized a fifth taste: umami. Umami is best described as savory or rich. You can taste umami in foods such as tomatoes, meat, soy, and Parmesan cheese.

UMAMI
IS THE JAPANESE WORD FOR
"YUMMY."

Today we know that taste is more complicated. The map idea is wrong. Taste buds all over your tongue and mouth can taste sweet, sour, bitter, salty, and umami.

The tongue has more than 10,000 taste buds!

EXPERIMENT

Taste is all about the **chemicals** that make up food interacting with your taste buds. But for that to happen, there's an important ingredient you need: saliva. (Yep, spit.) Saliva helps dissolve food chemicals so that your taste buds can actually taste them. To see how this works, try this experiment!

CRACKERS + WATER + PAPER TOWELS

1 Gather some crackers, a glass of drinking water, and some clean paper towels.

2 Use a paper towel to dry your tongue. Then, in small bites, eat a cracker. (It might not be easy to do!)

3 Take a drink of water and then eat another cracker. What's different this time? You should notice that it's easier to taste the cracker when your mouth is wet.

AROMA

Aroma is another word for scent or smell. Your sense of smell plays a big role in how food tastes. Think of a time you had a cold. When you can't breathe through your nose, it's difficult to taste food. If your nasal passages are clear, air is forced through them when you chew. Odor **molecules** in food come in contact with receptors at the opening of your nasal passages. Like taste buds, these receptors send messages to your brain about the food you're eating.

Try this experiment to see (or smell!) how aroma affects taste. Pinch your nose and eat an apple slice. Eat a second apple slice, but this time, don't pinch your nose. This time, the apple taste should be much stronger. Try this at your next meal. Notice how pinching your nose affects a food's taste.

TEXTURE

Texture is how food feels. Some words that could be used to describe a food's texture are creamy, crunchy, rough, smooth, fizzy, chewy, hard, crumbly, and fluffy. Can you think of any more words that describe texture?

Texture, like taste and aroma, helps your brain understand what you're eating. Think of baby food. Most baby food is soft and mushy. Because it's all a similar texture, you'd have a hard time figuring out exactly what you're eating. Apple puree tastes a lot like pear puree. But served fresh or left whole, apples and pears have different textures when you chew them.

People tend to like some textures and dislike others. Which textures do you like best?

How a food is prepared affects its texture. Oatmeal is a good example of this. Instant oatmeal is made up of the same ingredients whether you cook it for one minute or three minutes. But the cooking time affects the texture. Oatmeal cooked for one minute will be thin and watery. Oatmeal cooked for three minutes will be thick and mushy. Cook the oatmeal even longer and it becomes dry and really sticky. The different texture might affect whether you like oatmeal!

Explore texture with the oatmeal recipes on pages 50–52!

Flavor is all about the messages that are sent to your brain from your senses. In addition to taste, aroma, and texture, scientists have discovered other surprising factors that can affect those messages. Here are some of them:

TASTE + AROMA + TEXTURE = FLAVOR

Let's put it into action. Choose a food you like and a food you don't like. Write them on the lines below. Then for each food, choose a couple of words to describe its taste, aroma, and texture. (Examples are provided if you need inspiration.) Write the adjectives in the boxes.

	FOOD YOU LIKE: _____	FOOD YOU DON'T LIKE: _____
TASTE salty, sweet, bitter, umami, sour		
AROMA sweet, strong, fresh, spicy, etc.		
TEXTURE crunchy, soft, creamy, chewy, etc.		

What do you notice about your answers? If you change something about a food you dislike (such as its texture) is it possible you'd actually like it? For instance, you might not like cauliflower, but would that change if it was served crispy instead of soft? It's worth a try!

FOOD ALLERGIES & INTOLERANCES

Sometimes even if a person likes a certain food, she can't eat it (or in some cases, touch it) because of a food allergy or food intolerance.

To understand food allergies, it helps to know a little about your body's immune system. The immune system is a network of cells, tissues, and organs that work together to protect your body from illness. When germs enter your body, your immune system will go into action to fight off the germs. Sometimes this will cause uncomfortable symptoms. For example, if you've ever been sick with the flu, you may have had a fever. A fever can be one result of your immune system attacking harmful germs.

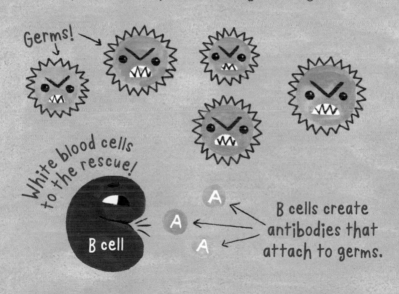

Germs!

White blood cells to the rescue!

B cell

A A A

B cells create antibodies that attach to germs.

The antibodies let other cells know to attack the germs.

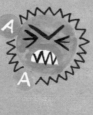

Like this!

White blood cell

A **food allergy** is when a person's immune system mistakes what is typically a harmless ingredient for something harmful that it needs to fight. As a result, people who have food allergies get sick—sometimes very sick—from eating certain foods. Some common food allergies are to nuts, eggs, wheat, soy, and dairy.

People can't predict whether they'll develop food allergies. Many people who have them are born with them or develop them over time. Medicine can sometimes help people who have certain food allergies, but it's much better (and much safer!) for them to avoid the foods in the first place.

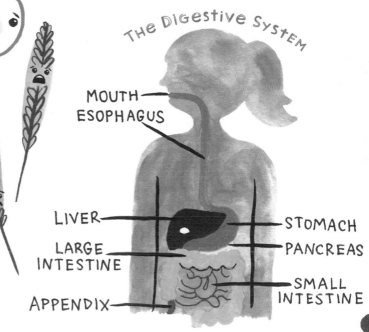

The Digestive System

MOUTH
ESOPHAGUS

LIVER

LARGE INTESTINE

APPENDIX

STOMACH

PANCREAS

SMALL INTESTINE

A **food intolerance** is when a person has trouble digesting a certain food or ingredient. She might get a stomach ache after eating it. Food allergies affect the immune system, and food intolerances affect the digestive system. Some common food intolerances are to gluten, dairy, and eggs.

Gluten is a mixture of proteins that are found in most grains such as wheat, barley, and rye. This means that most breads, bakery products, and cereals contain gluten. If a person is not able to digest gluten, she needs to either avoid these types of foods or use recipes with ingredients that don't contain gluten.

Turn to page 87 for a gluten-free chocolate chip cookie recipe and page 68 for a gluten-free bread recipe!

RECIPE LOGBOOK

Keep track of the recipes you try and rate them as you go! Then write two or three words to help you remember how each recipe turned out.

RECIPE	MADE IT!	STAR RATING	WORDS TO TO DESCRIBE IT
Fried Eggs		☆☆☆☆☆	
Scrambled Eggs		☆☆☆☆☆	
Butter		☆☆☆☆☆	
Whipped Cream		☆☆☆☆☆	
Ice Cream		☆☆☆☆☆	
Sorbet		☆☆☆☆☆	
Chocolate Candy Shell		☆☆☆☆☆	
Strawberry Sauce		☆☆☆☆☆	
Sunrise Smoothie		☆☆☆☆☆	
Peanut Butter Banana Smoothie		☆☆☆☆☆	
Berry Cherry Smoothie		☆☆☆☆☆	
Microwave Oatmeal		☆☆☆☆☆	
Overnight Oatmeal		☆☆☆☆☆	
Baked Oatmeal		☆☆☆☆☆	
Fruit Salsa		☆☆☆☆☆	

RECIPE	MADE IT!	STAR RATING	WORDS TO TO DESCRIBE IT
Hummus		☆☆☆☆☆	
Pancakes		☆☆☆☆☆	
Banana Bread		☆☆☆☆☆	
Gluten-Free Bread		☆☆☆☆☆	
Overnight Bread		☆☆☆☆☆	
Pizza		☆☆☆☆☆	
Gluten-Free Pizza Crust		☆☆☆☆☆	
Melba Sandwich		☆☆☆☆☆	
Rainbow Crunch Sandwich		☆☆☆☆☆	
Chewy Chocolate Chip Cookies		☆☆☆☆☆	
Crispy Chocolate Chip Cookies		☆☆☆☆☆	
Cakey Chocolate Chip Cookies		☆☆☆☆☆	
Gluten-Free Chocolate Chip Cookies		☆☆☆☆☆	
Vanilla Cake		☆☆☆☆☆	
Flourless Chocolate Cake		☆☆☆☆☆	
Buttercream Frosting		☆☆☆☆☆	
Chocolate Bark		☆☆☆☆☆	

FRIED EGGS

FOOD SCIENCE

 Ask an adult to help you with this recipe.

INGREDIENTS
- Nonstick cooking spray
- 2 eggs
- ¼ teaspoon salt
- ¼ teaspoon pepper

PROTEINS
EVAPORATION
COAGULATION

DIRECTIONS

1. Spray a small frying pan with nonstick cooking spray. Place the pan on a burner that's turned off.

2. Crack two eggs into the pan. Sprinkle salt and pepper over the eggs.

3. Cover the pan, and ask an adult to turn the burner to low heat.

4. Check the eggs after 5 minutes. They're ready when a faint white film forms over the egg yolks. If you don't like runny eggs, cook them for an additional 1–2 minutes. Use a spatula to transfer the eggs to a plate.

This type of egg is called "sunny-side up." Because it's only cooked on one side, the yolk stays round and yellow like a sun.

SCRAMBLED EGGS

FOOD SCIENCE

 Ask an adult to help you with this recipe.

INGREDIENTS
- 2 eggs
- 1 tablespoon milk
- ¼ teaspoon salt
- ¼ teaspoon pepper
- Nonstick cooking spray

**PROTEINS
EVAPORATION
COAGULATION**

DIRECTIONS

1. Crack the eggs into a small mixing bowl. Whisk the eggs until the yolks and whites are blended together, about 1 minute.

2. Add the milk, salt, and pepper, and whisk again.

3. Spray a small frying pan with nonstick cooking spray. Place the pan on a burner, and ask an adult to turn the burner to low heat. Let the pan warm up for about 2 minutes.

4. Slowly pour the egg mixture into the pan. Use a plastic or wooden spatula to push the eggs around in the pan every 30 seconds or so. As soon as the egg mixture becomes solid, turn off the burner. Use a spatula to transfer the eggs to a plate.

Egg yolks can be pale yellow, deep orange, or any shade in between! And the shells of chicken eggs can come in many colors—even light blue or pale pink. The yolk and shell colors depend on the breed of the chicken that laid it and the type of food she ate.

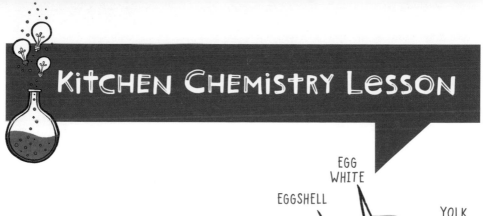

KITCHEN CHEMISTRY LESSON

EGGS are made up of water and proteins. **Protein** is a type of **nutrient** that supplies energy and helps build muscle. It helps give food its structure and texture.

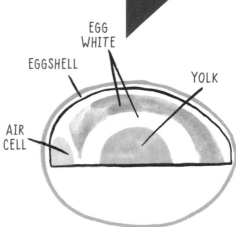

EGG WHITE

EGGSHELL

YOLK

AIR CELL

When an egg is cooked, the water in the egg heats up and is released into the air. This is called **evaporation;** it's when a liquid changes to a vapor. The loss of the water makes the proteins in the egg join more tightly together and changes the egg's texture. This is called **coagulation.** If you cook eggs for too long, they lose too much water and the texture becomes rubbery.

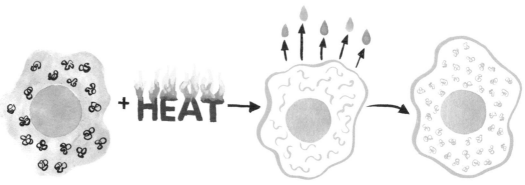

An uncooked egg has a lot of water.

Heat causes the water to evaporate.

The proteins that are left behind join together.

BUTTER

 Ask an adult to help you with this recipe.

INGREDIENTS

EMULSIONS

- 2 cups (16 ounces) heavy whipping cream
- ⅛ teaspoon salt

DIRECTIONS

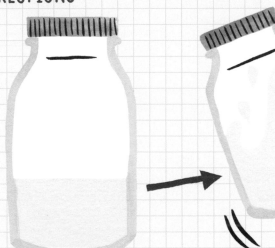

1. Pour the cream into a 1-quart mason jar. Screw the lid on the jar tightly.

2. Shake the jar for 20–25 minutes. It helps to make this recipe with friends so you can take turns shaking the jar. (Turning on music also helps!) After the first 15 minutes, solid clumps will start to form in the cream. These are called curds. Keep shaking and the curds will eventually stick together in much larger clumps. This is the butter!

Find the recipe for this bread on page 72!

3. Stop shaking the jar once there is a large solid clump of butter. Hold a mesh strainer over a small mixing bowl and scrape the butter into the strainer. The liquid that drains into the bowl is buttermilk. (You can save this in a sealed container in the refrigerator and use it for recipes such as the pancakes on page 62.)

4. Fill a measuring cup with 2 cups cold water. Place the butter in a small mixing bowl. Pour ½ cup of the water into the bowl with the butter. Knead the butter with your hands until the water turns cloudy. Dump out the cloudy water, keeping the butter in the bowl. Repeat the process, adding ½ cup of water at a time, until you've used all the water.

5. Sprinkle the salt on the butter and knead it again until the salt is mixed in. Store the butter in a sealed container in the refrigerator for up to a week.

Try this! To speed up this recipe, skip steps 1 and 2 and ask an adult to pour the cream into a food processor. Ask the adult to run the food processor on high for about 4 minutes. Then move on to step 3.

WHIPPED CREAM

INGREDIENTS

EMULSIONS

- 1 cup (8 ounces) heavy cream or heavy whipping cream
- 2 tablespoons granulated sugar
- ½ teaspoon vanilla extract

DIRECTIONS

1. Place a 1-quart mason jar in the freezer for 15 minutes. Remove the jar from the freezer and pour the heavy cream into it. Add the sugar and vanilla extract. Put the lid tightly on the jar.

2. Shake the jar for 5 minutes.

3. After 5 minutes, check the cream. If you dip a spoon into it and it's thick and creamy, it's ready. If not, put the lid back on and continuing shaking for a minute or two. (But be careful not to shake it too long or it will turn into sweet vanilla butter!)

Like the butter recipe, it helps if you make this recipe with friends so that you can take turns shaking the jar!

KiTCHEN CHEMISTRY LeSSON

When you make butter or whipped cream, you change a liquid to a semisolid. For this to happen, the cream needs to be at least 30 percent **fat.** (That's why you can't make butter or whipped cream with milk.)

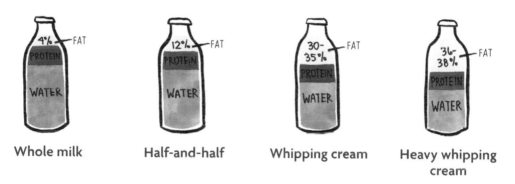

| Whole milk | Half-and-half | Whipping cream | Heavy whipping cream |

When you whip liquid cream, tiny air bubbles form in it. The bubbles get trapped between bits of fat and the barriers around the fat break down. The liquid cream becomes a foam called an emulsion. An **emulsion** is a mixture of different substances that don't normally mix (such as the air and the fat).

Ice Cream

 Ask an adult to help you with this recipe.

INGREDIENTS

- 1 (12-ounce) can evaporated milk
- 1 cup powdered sugar
- 2 teaspoons vanilla extract

**EMULSIONS
FREEZING**

DIRECTIONS

1. Place the evaporated milk in the refrigerator overnight. Once chilled, pour the milk into a blender. Ask an adult to blend on high for 45 seconds. Add the powdered sugar and vanilla extract. Blend on high for 30 seconds.

2. Pour the mixture into a food storage container, cover, and place in the freezer for 1 hour. After 1 hour, remove the container and use a whisk to stir the mixture a few times. Place the container back in the freezer.

3. Repeat the freezing and stirring in step 2 two more times. Then freeze the mixture overnight. The final texture of the ice cream will be somewhat soft. Scoop some into a bowl to enjoy, or store the ice cream in a covered container in the freezer.

For chocolate ice cream, use 1 tablespoon cocoa powder instead of the vanilla extract.

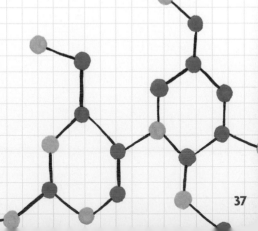

SORBET

 Ask an adult to help you with this recipe.

INGREDIENTS

- ½ cup apple juice
- 1 tablespoon frozen orange juice concentrate
- 1 (12-ounce) bag frozen mango chunks
- ½ cup water

PECTIN
FIBER
FREEZING

DIRECTIONS

1. Place the apple juice, orange juice concentrate, and half of the mango chunks in a blender. Ask an adult to blend on high for a few seconds at a time until smooth.

2. Add the water and the rest of the fruit to the blender. Ask an adult to blend on high for a few seconds at a time until smooth.

3. Place the sorbet in a covered container. Freeze the sorbet for 1–2 hours or until it's hard enough to scoop.

To make strawberry banana sorbet, use ½ cup frozen strawberries and 1 frozen banana instead of orange juice concentrate and mango.

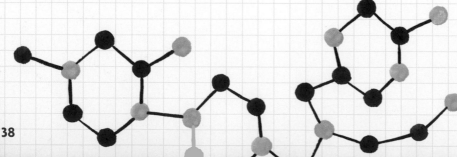

Kitchen Chemistry Lesson

MAKING ICE CREAM

SUGAR
FLAVORING
CREAM
AIR

UNSTIRRED ☹
↓
Large ice crystals
⇓
Too solid & gritty

STIRRED ☺
↓
Breaks into small ice crystals
⇓
Smooth & delicious

1 CREATE BASE   **2** CREATE EMULSION   **3** FREEZE AND STIR

ICE CREAM

Most store-bought ice cream is made using an ice cream maker. It's a special machine that constantly churns the ice cream base as it freezes. In the recipe on page 37, the ice cream base is stirred by hand instead of churned in a machine. The texture won't be as smooth, but the stirring re-creates what an ice cream maker does to the mixture.

EXPERIMENT

Cold temperatures can numb your taste buds. This means that ice cream often gets a lot of extra sugar added to it. Plus, most ice cream is made up of a LOT of air, anywhere from 30%–50%. (More air equals creamier ice cream.) Do a taste experiment! Let a little ice cream melt in a bowl. Then taste the melted ice cream and ice cream straight from the freezer. The melted ice cream that doesn't have air in it will taste much sweeter.

KITCHEN CHEMISTRY LESSON

MAKING SORBET

1 FREEZE FRUIT *For best texture*

Berries
Peaches
Bananas
Mangoes

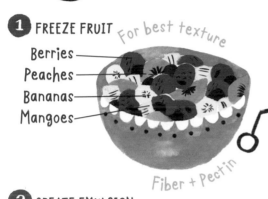

Fiber + Pectin

Fiber is a carbohydrate the body can't digest. Instead, it helps move along other foods in the digestive system.

2 CREATE EMULSION

JUICE { WATER
SUGAR

FRUIT

CO_2CH_3

Pectin is a starch, a type of carbohydrate that exists naturally in fruit. Pectin gives fruit its structure.

HO

OH

A **carbohydrate** is a nutrient that gives the body energy.

3 FREEZE The final step is freezing the sorbet base. Unlike ice cream, the sorbet in our recipe doesn't need to be stirred. The pectin and fiber in the fruit prevent ice crystals from easily forming (like stirring does in ice cream). After a couple of hours in the freezer, the sorbet should be firm enough to scoop.

When pectin freezes, it breaks down the cell walls in the fruit and creates a gel-like substance. This is what makes sorbet smooth—and also makes smoothies creamy.

CHOCOLATE CANDY SHELL
ICE CREAM TOPPING

FOOD SCIENCE

 Ask an adult to help you with this recipe.

INGREDIENTS
- 2 cups chocolate chips
- 6 tablespoons coconut oil

**MELTING POINT
FREEZING POINT
FATS**

DIRECTIONS

1. Place the chocolate chips and coconut oil in a microwave-safe bowl and stir together.

2. Ask an adult to heat the mixture in a microwave on high for 1–2 minutes, stirring every 30 seconds until melted. Stir the mixture until it's smooth. Then let it cool slightly.

3. Pour the chocolate over ice cream. It will harden and form a candy shell! Store leftover topping at room temperature in a sealed container. If it hardens, reheat the topping for 10–15 seconds to melt it again.

250
APPROX.

200

150

Kitchen Chemistry Lesson

85°
HEATING

85°
COOLING

What happened? It helps to understand something called the melting point. The **melting point** is the temperature at which a substance changes from a solid to a liquid. (The **freezing point** is the temperature at which a substance changes from a liquid to a solid.) Now let's consider the ingredients.

COCOA POWDER

SUGAR

COCOA BUTTER

Chocolate chips are made from cocoa powder, sugar, and a fat called cocoa butter. Depending on how much cocoa butter (fat) is in the chocolate, the melting point of chocolate is about 85 degrees Fahrenheit.

Coconut oil comes from the white "meat" inside coconuts. Compared to other oils such as olive oil or vegetable oil, coconut oil is high in fat. The large amount of fat causes the oil to have a melting point of about 76 degrees Fahrenheit. (This is much higher than water and most oils.) Most of the time, coconut oil is a soft paste. If it's stored in a warm place, the paste turns into a liquid.

Most ice cream is between five degrees and ten degrees when it's served. When the melted chocolate and coconut oil mixture is poured on cold ice cream, the candy freezes very quickly. (Remember, the temperature doesn't have to drop very much for coconut oil to turn to a solid. The cold ice cream speeds up this process.)

Strawberry Sauce
ICE CREAM TOPPING

FOOD SCIENCE

 Ask an adult to help you with this recipe.

INGREDIENTS
- 1 pound fresh strawberries
- 1 tablespoon granulated sugar

**SUGARS
MACERATION**

DIRECTIONS

1. Wash and drain the strawberries. Ask an adult to remove the tops and cut the strawberries into quarters.

2. Place the cut strawberries in a large microwave-safe bowl, and stir in the sugar. Let the berries and sugar sit at room temperature for about 30 minutes.

3. After 30 minutes, stir the strawberries. Place the strawberries in a microwave and heat on high for 1–2 minutes, stirring after each minute. Use a pastry cutter or potato masher to crush the strawberries, and stir again. Serve the strawberry sauce warm over ice cream.

What happened? Adding sugar to fresh strawberries causes a chemical process called maceration. **Maceration** is when you soften something (often fruit) by soaking it in a liquid. When you add sugar to strawberries, it causes the berries to release their own liquid. (Strawberries are 92 percent water!) The result is softened berries in a sweet syrup. Heating the berries in the microwave softens the berries even more.

92% WATER

LOOK OUT BELOW!

CANNONBALL!

I'M GOING IN!

THANKS SUGAR!

SWEET!

KiTCHEN CHEMiSTRY LeSSON

SMOOTHIE HOW-TO

Smoothies can be a healthy breakfast or a delicious snack. For a great tasting smoothie, make sure your recipe includes at least one item from each of the following categories:

LIQUID INGREDIENTS

Why? Liquid ingredients help the solid ingredients blend together more easily and prevent the blender blades from getting stuck.

CREAMY INGREDIENTS

Why? The fat and fiber in these ingredients help increase a smoothie's **viscosity.** That's another way of saying they make the smoothie thick and creamy.

THE PERFECT SMOOTHIE!

COLD INGREDIENTS

Why? Adding ice or other frozen ingredients makes the smoothie cold and frosty.

FOLLOW THESE INSTRUCTIONS TO BUILD A BETTER SMOOTHIE!

1 Build a good smoothie from the bottom up! Always start with the liquid ingredients. This will help the blender's blades to spin freely and not get stuck.

2 Next, add the creamy ingredients such as yogurt, fresh fruit, avocado, or peanut butter.

3 Finish with any frozen ingredients such as frozen fruit or ice.

4 The last step is to blend the ingredients until everything is smooth! Blending incorporates air into the ingredients, making an emulsion.

Smoothies

 Ask an adult to help you with this recipe.

SUNRISE SMOOTHIE

Place the following ingredients in a blender: ½ cup milk, ½ teaspoon vanilla extract, ¼ cup vanilla Greek yogurt, 1 teaspoon honey, 2 tablespoons frozen orange juice concentrate, and ½ cup frozen peaches. Ask an adult to blend on high until smooth.

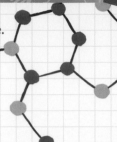

EMULSION VISCOSITY

PEANUT BUTTER BANANA SMOOTHIE

Place the following ingredients in a blender: ½ cup almond milk, ¼ cup vanilla Greek yogurt, 1 tablespoon peanut butter, and ½ of a frozen banana. Ask an adult to blend on high until smooth.

BERRY CHERRY SMOOTHIE

Place the following ingredients in a blender: ½ cup milk, 1 tablespoon cranberry juice, ½ cup vanilla Greek yogurt, 1 teaspoon honey, ½ cup frozen sweet cherries (with no pits), and ¼ cup frozen strawberries. Ask an adult to blend on high until smooth.

Kitchen Chemistry Lesson

OatMEAL

is ground oats, a type of cereal grain. Oatmeal is available in a few different forms. The most common types are:

QUICK OATS

Oats that have been steamed, rolled thin, and cut into pieces. They will cook quickly but have a less hearty texture. Also called "instant oats."

ROLLED OATS

Oats that have been steamed and rolled thin but not cut into pieces. Also called "old-fashioned oats."

STEEL-CUT OATS

Oats that have been cut into a few pieces but not steamed and rolled flat. These oats take the longest to cook.

Oats have an outer shell called a membrane.

HEAT

Heat breaks down the membrane.

And the oat becomes soft.

49

MICROWAVE OATMEAL

INGREDIENTS

- ¼ cup quick oats
- ½ cup water
- 1 tablespoon mix-ins
  (dried cranberries, raisins, nuts)
- 1 teaspoon honey
- 1 teaspoon milk

**ABSORPTION
STARCH**

DIRECTIONS

1. Pour oats, water, and mix-ins into a microwave-safe bowl.

2. Place in the microwave and heat on high for 45–60 seconds.

3. Stir in honey; then add the milk. Top with fresh fruit or granola!

Watch the oatmeal carefully as it cooks. If you cook the oatmeal for too long, too much water will evaporate and the oatmeal will become thick and sticky. Oatmeal also gets thicker as it cools. So remove it while it looks a little underdone!

OVERNIGHT OATMEAL

INGREDIENTS
- ½ cup quick oats
- ½ cup milk (almond milk and soy milk can be used)
- ¼ cup plain Greek yogurt
- 2 teaspoons jam or honey
- ¼ cup fresh fruit

ABSORPTION STARCH

DIRECTIONS

1. Place oats, milk, yogurt, and jam or honey in jar. With the lid tightly screwed on, shake the jar for about 30 seconds to mix the ingredients.

2. Add the fresh fruit to the jar and stir until mixed.

3. Place the lid back on the jar and place the jar in the refrigerator overnight. In the morning, the oatmeal will be ready to eat—no heating required!

Heat isn't the only thing that can break down oats' outer membrane. Soaking oats in liquid will also do the trick!

Baked Oatmeal

FOOD SCIENCE

 Ask an adult to help you with this recipe.

INGREDIENTS
- Nonstick cooking spray
- 1½ cups rolled oats
- 1½ cups sliced strawberries
- ⅓ cup light brown sugar
- pinch of salt
- ¼ teaspoon cinnamon
- 1 egg
- 1¾ cups milk
- 2 tablesp oons unsalted butter, melted and cooled

ABSORPTION STARCH

DIRECTIONS

1. Preheat oven to 350 degrees. Coat a 2-quart baking dish with nonstick cooking spray.

2. Pour oats into the baking dish. Layer the strawberries on top of the oats.

3. In a mixing bowl, whisk together the brown sugar, salt, cinnamon, egg, milk, and butter. Pour the mixture into the baking dish. Gently stir to combine the liquid ingredients with the dry ingredients.

4. Bake the oatmeal in the oven for 25–30 minutes. Ask an adult to test the oatmeal to see if it's done by using an oven mitt to gently shake the baking dish. The oatmeal is done when it's set in the middle and doesn't move when you shake the dish. Let the oatmeal cool slightly before serving.

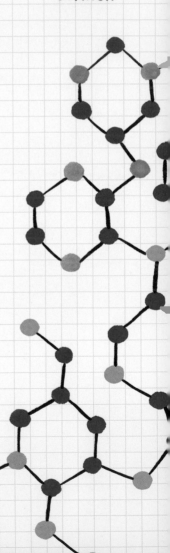

Top with
maple
syrup!

Fruit Salsa

 Ask an adult to help you with this recipe.

INGREDIENTS
- 1 tablespoon lemon juice
- 1 tablespoon honey
- ½ teaspoon vanilla extract
- 1½ cups sliced strawberries
- ½ cup diced fresh pineapple

**MACERATION
MAILLARD
REACTION**

DIRECTIONS
1. In a serving bowl, stir together the lemon juice, honey, and vanilla extract.

2. Stir in the strawberries and pineapple until they're coated with the lemon juice mixture.

3. Cover the bowl and chill for 1 hour in the refrigerator before serving. Serve with pita chips or crackers, or try the cinnamon sticks recipe below!

CINNAMON STICKS
Cut a few slices of bread into strips that are about 1 inch wide. In a small bowl, mix together ¼ cup granulated sugar and 1 tablespoon cinnamon. Ask an adult to heat a small frying pan on medium heat and melt about a tablespoon of butter in the pan. Use a spatula to place the bread strips in the pan. Cook for a couple of minutes on each side until the strips are brown and crispy. Ask an adult to help you remove them from the pan and roll them in the cinnamon sugar mixture. Let the cinnamon sticks cool slightly before eating.

HUMMUS

FOOD SCIENCE

 ★ **Ask an adult to help you with this recipe.**

INGREDIENTS

- 1 (15-ounce) can chickpeas
- 3 tablespoons tahini paste
- 1 tablespoon lemon juice
- 2 tablespoons olive oil
- ½ teaspoon cumin
- 1 teaspoon minced garlic
- salt and pepper
- ¼ cup water

FIBER
CELLULOSE

DIRECTIONS

1. Drain the chickpeas by pouring them into a colander in a sink. Rinse the chickpeas in the colander for about 15 seconds.

2. Place all the ingredients in a blender in the order listed.

3. Ask an adult to blend on high until smooth. If the mixture isn't blending, add an extra tablespoon of water and blend again.

4. Scoop the hummus into a bowl and serve with fresh veggies. Refrigerate leftovers for up to five days.

For extra smooth and tasty hummus, follow the tip on the next page! Or if you're in a hurry, move ahead to step 2.

Kitchen Chemistry Lesson

The secret to smooth hummus is in the chickpeas. Canned chickpeas still have their outer skins. The skins are made of a plant fiber called **cellulose**. It's safe to eat but won't blend as smoothly as the chickpea itself. For the smoothest hummus, try this before adding the chickpeas to the blender:

1. Fill a mixing bowl halfway with water.

2. Pour the colander of rinsed chickpeas into the bowl of water.

3. Rub the chickpeas between your fingers. The skins should come off and float to the surface. Keep rubbing the chickpeas and scooping the skins out of the water until most of the skins are gone.

Move on to step 2 in the hummus recipe!

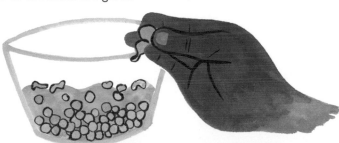

Kitchen Chemistry Lesson

ALL ABOUT BAKING

Baking seems like a magic trick. Ingredients go in the oven looking one way, and come out as something new and different. But whether you're making bread, pizza crust, or cookies, baking involves a lot of scientific know-how.

Part of learning to bake is learning how ingredients work together. Here are some common baking ingredients and what they do.

Butter and shortening are fats and add moisture, flavor, and texture to baked goods. Butter melts at a lower temperature than shortening, so it spreads more when baked.

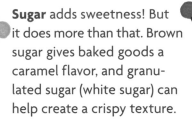

Vanilla extract adds vanilla flavor to a dough or batter and brings out the other flavors.

Sugar adds sweetness! But it does more than that. Brown sugar gives baked goods a caramel flavor, and granulated sugar (white sugar) can help create a crispy texture.

Salt acts as a flavor booster. It not only adds saltiness but also intensifies other flavors, including sweetness. In bread dough, salt works with gluten to strengthen the bread's structure.

Flour holds together all the other ingredients in a dough or batter. All-purpose flour is the most common type of flour, but there are many different types of flours.

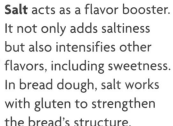

Eggs help fats (such as butter or shortening) bind together with liquid ingredients and help give baked goods their shape. They also add a richer flavor and lighter texture.

In any baking recipe you'll usually end up with either a dough or a batter.

Dough is a flour-and-liquid mixture that is thick and sturdy enough to be shaped.

Batter is a flour-and-liquid mixture that is thin enough to pour (think pancakes and brownies).

Not an actual leavening agent

WHY DO DOUGH AND BATTER RISE?

Both dough and batter need an ingredient called a leavening agent. A **leavening agent** is something that introduces air into dough or batter and helps it to expand and rise. If you look closely at a slice of sandwich bread, you'll notice that bread is full of tiny holes. The holes were created by a leavening agent releasing **carbon dioxide**.

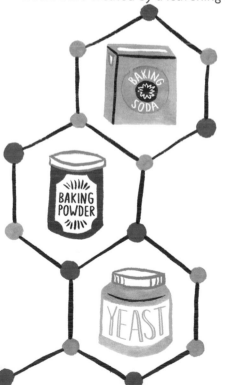

THE MOST COMMON LEAVENING AGENTS:

Baking soda is also called sodium bicarbonate. When it's heated or mixed with an acid, it releases a gas called carbon dioxide and creates bubbles in dough or batter. (These are the same gas bubbles you see in soda and other carbonated drinks.)

Baking powder is baking soda (sodium bicarbonate) mixed with an **acid** such as cream of tarter. Like baking soda, it produces a **chemical reaction** in the dough or batter, but it's not as powerful.

Yeast is made up of small, single-cell organisms that feed on sugars. As the yeast feeds on sugars in dough, it gives off carbon dioxide, which expands the dough by creating tiny air pockets.

BREAD

Bread can be divided into three main categories:

YEAST BREADS
These breads use yeast as their leavening agent.

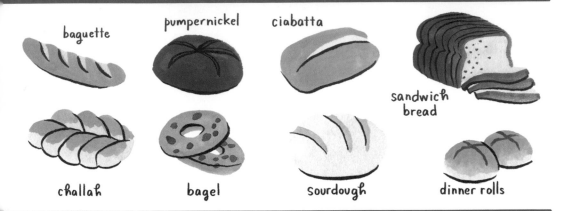

baguette

pumpernickel

ciabatta

sandwich bread

challah

bagel

sourdough

dinner rolls

QUICK BREADS
These breads use baking soda or baking powder as their leavening agent.

pancakes

muffin

soda bread

banana bread

pumpkin bread

biscuits

corn bread

waffle

FLATBREADS

These flat, thin breads either don't use a leavening agent or use a very small amount.

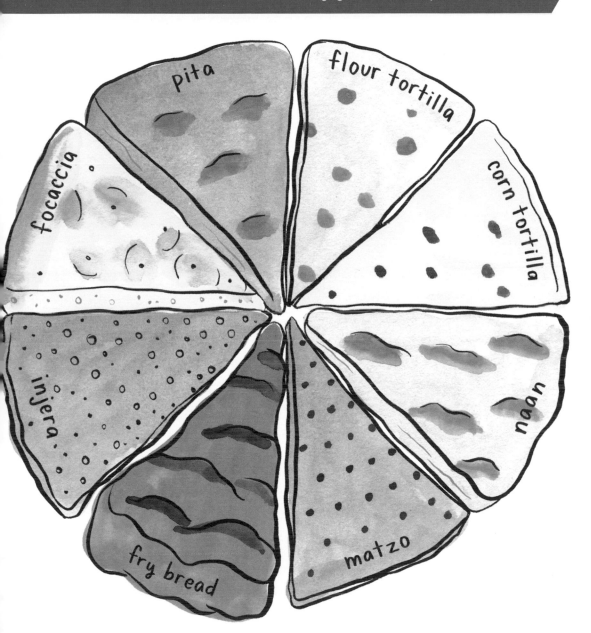

PANCAKES

FOOD SCIENCE

 Ask an adult to help you with this recipe.

INGREDIENTS

LEAVENING

- 4 tablespoons unsalted butter
- 1⅔ cups all-purpose flour
- 1 tablespoon granulated sugar
- 1 teaspoon baking soda
- ½ teaspoon salt
- 1 egg
- 1¼ cups buttermilk
- Nonstick cooking spray
- Toppings

DIRECTIONS

1. Melt the butter in a small saucepan on the stove, using low heat.

2. In a medium-size bowl, use a whisk to mix together the flour, sugar, baking soda, and salt. In a large bowl, whisk the egg; then whisk in the buttermilk and melted butter. Pour the dry ingredients into the wet ingredients in the large bowl, and whisk the batter until just mixed. It's fine to have some small lumps.

3. Coat a skillet or griddle with cooking spray. Ask an adult to set it on the stove, and turn the burner to medium heat. When the pan is hot, dip into the batter with a ¼ cup measuring cup and pour the batter onto the pan. Space the pancakes so they don't touch—try only one or two at first.

4. When bubbles have formed in the pancake, test it with a spatula to see if it's firm enough to flip.

5. When the pancake is ready, flip it over and let it cook 1 minute on the other side. Slip the spatula tip into the center of the pancake. If it comes out clean, the pancake is done. Cook the remaining batter, following steps 3–5. Serve the pancakes hot with your favorite toppings.

BANANA BREAD

 Ask an adult to help you with this recipe.

INGREDIENTS
- Nonstick cooking spray
- 3 ripe bananas (about 1 cup)
- ½ cup butter, softened
- ½ cup granulated sugar
- ¼ cup brown sugar
- 1 egg, beaten
- 1 teaspoon vanilla extract
- 1½ cups all-purpose flour
- 2 teaspoons baking powder
- pinch of salt

DIRECTIONS

1. Preheat oven to 350 degrees. Coat a 9-by-5-inch loaf pan with cooking spray.

2. In a mixing bowl, mash the ripe bananas with a fork until smooth. Then add the softened butter, sugars, egg, and vanilla extract to the mashed bananas. Stir until combined.

3. In a separate bowl, mix together the flour, baking powder, and salt. Add the flour mixture to the banana mixture and stir until combined.

4. Pour the batter into the loaf pan. Ask an adult to bake the bread for about 50 minutes or until a toothpick inserted in the center comes out clean.

5. Ask an adult to remove the bread from the oven and let it cool in the pan for about 20 minutes. Then remove the banana bread from the pan and let it cool on a wire rack before serving.

LEAVENING

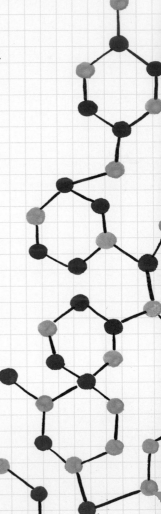

Turn to the next page for this gluten-free bread recipe!

Kitchen Chemistry Lesson

We learned about gluten on page 23. Many kinds of bread have gluten. This is because gluten is a protein that's found in wheat-based flours such as whole wheat flour, all-purpose flour, and cake flour. Gluten plays a big role in recipes because it has three main jobs:

1. It's a binder. This means it helps the dough stick together.

We stick together!

2. It gives the dough elasticity. This means the dough can be stretched and shaped.

3. It gives bread structure and shape.

If you want to make bread that doesn't have gluten, you need to use other ingredients that will perform these three jobs.

In the gluten-free bread recipe on the next page, the binder is made of flaxseed meal and water. This paste keeps the dough's ingredients together and makes the bread moist.

GLUTEN-FREE BREAD

 Ask an adult to help you with this recipe.

INGREDIENTS

- 2 cups brown rice flour
- 1 cup buckwheat flour
- 1 cup plus 3 tablespoons quick oats (gluten-free)
- 1 tablespoon baking soda
- 1 teaspoon salt
- 1 tablespoon active dry yeast

- ¼ cup warm water
- 1 tablespoon coconut oil or butter
- ½ cup buttermilk
- 4 tablespoons flaxseed meal
- 8 tablespoons water
- 1 cup water

LEAVENING
BINDER

} These ingredients are used to make the binder.

DIRECTIONS

2. In a separate bowl, stir the yeast into ¼ cup warm water. Let it sit for 10 minutes until the yeast bubbles.

1. In a large mixing bowl, combine the brown rice flour, buckwheat flour, 1 cup quick oats, baking soda, and salt.

3. Grease a loaf pan with coconut oil or butter, and sprinkle with 3 tablespoons quick oats.

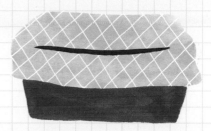

4. Ask an adult to help you make the binder: In a small saucepan, stir together the flaxseed meal and 8 tablespoons of water. Cook on low heat, stirring occasionally. The binder is finished when it turns into a sticky paste. This should take a few minutes. Remove the pan from the stove, and let the binder cool.

6. Pour the bread mixture into the loaf pan. Place a towel over the pan to let the bread rise a little while you preheat the oven to 350 degrees (about 20 minutes).

The dough will be wet and sticky and look like cake batter.

5. Add the yeast mixture, buttermilk, and binder to the flour mixture. Stir until combined. Then stir in the cup of water.

7. Bake the bread for 50 minutes. Turn the oven off and leave the bread inside until it's completely cooled. Ask an adult to help you remove the bread from the pan.

KitCHEN CHEMiStRY LESSON

KNEAD TO KNOW

Recipes that call for yeast—such as baguettes or pizza crust—will usually require you to knead the dough before you bake it. Kneading is a process that introduces air into the dough and stretches out the gluten fibers so the dough can rise. Here's how to do it!

1 Start with clean, dry hands. Sprinkle a little flour on a clean work surface such as a cutting board or countertop.

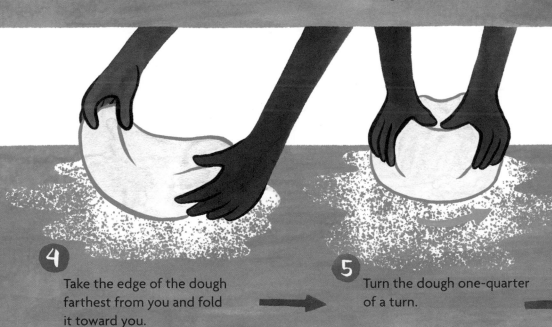

4 Take the edge of the dough farthest from you and fold it toward you.

5 Turn the dough one-quarter of a turn.

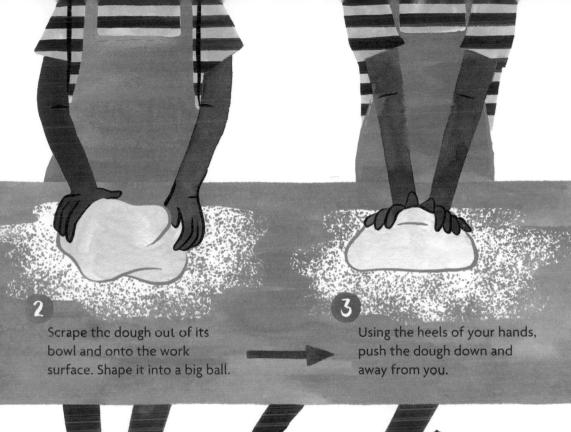

2 Scrape the dough out of its bowl and onto the work surface. Shape it into a big ball.

3 Using the heels of your hands, push the dough down and away from you.

6 Repeat steps 3–5. Follow your recipe to see how long to knead the dough. Depending on what you're making, it can be anywhere from a few seconds to 10 minutes.

If your hands get tired, ask a friend or family member to help!

OVERNIGHT BREAD

 Ask an adult to help you with this recipe.

INGREDIENTS

- 3 cups bread flour
- ½ tablespoon yeast
- 1 teaspoon salt
- 1 cup warm milk
- ½ cup warm water
- 1 tablespoon olive oil
- Nonstick cooking spray

LEAVENING

KNEADING

DIRECTIONS

The Night Before

1. Mix all the ingredients in a mixing bowl that will be big enough to hold the dough once it expands. (A 2-quart bowl works well.)

2. Once the yeast starts to bubble, cover the bowl with plastic wrap. Place the bowl in the refrigerator overnight.

This is a yeast bread that rises while you sleep!

The Next Day

3. Preheat the oven to 425 degrees. Spray a cookie sheet with nonstick cooking spray.

4. Remove the dough from the refrigerator. With clean hands, knead the dough for 10–12 minutes following the directions on pages 70–71.

5. Place the dough back into the bowl. Cover the bowl with a clean towel, and let the dough rest for 30 minutes at room temperature.

6. Place the dough on the baking sheet and shape into an oval, tucking the ends of the dough underneath.

7. Bake for 30–35 minutes. The bread is done when it's a dark golden brown. Ask an adult to remove the bread from the oven. Let the bread cool completely before serving.

PiZZA

 Ask an adult to help you with this recipe.

PIZZA CRUST INGREDIENTS

**LEAVENING
KNEADING**

- 1 cup warm water
- 2 teaspoons active dry yeast
- 1½ cups all-purpose flour
- 1 teaspoon salt
- 1 tablespoon olive oil
- 2 tablespoons cornmeal

DIRECTIONS

1. Pour the warm water into a small bowl and stir in the yeast. Let sit for 5 minutes.

2. In a mixing bowl, stir together the flour, salt, and olive oil. The mixture will be very dry and crumbly.

3. Pour the yeast mixture into the flour mixture. Stir until a soft dough forms. Put a little flour on your (clean!) hands and shape the dough into a ball.

4. Cover the bowl with plastic wrap. Let the dough rise for 1 hour.

5. Sprinkle some flour on a clean cutting board or countertop. Knead the dough a few times on the floured surface.

6. Lightly grease a 12-inch pizza pan with butter and sprinkle it with the cornmeal. Place the dough in the middle of the pan. Push, pull, and stretch the dough until it fills the pan.

7. Ask an adult to bake the crust in a preheated 400-degree oven for about 5 minutes.

ASSEMBLE THE PIZZA

1. After you've prebaked the crust, use a spoon to spread pizza sauce on top. For a 12-inch pizza, use about ½ cup of sauce.

2. Next comes the cheese. Sprinkle 1 cup of shredded mozzarella (or another shredded cheese) over the pizza sauce.

3. Finish off the pizza with toppings: pepperoni, mushrooms, tomatoes, or anything you'd like!

4. Ask an adult to bake the pizza in a preheated 400-degree oven for 15–17 minutes. The pizza is done when the cheese is melted and the edges of the crust are starting to turn brown.

GLUTEN-FREE PIZZA CRUST

FOOD SCIENCE

 Ask an adult to help you with this recipe.

INGREDIENTS

LEAVENING

- 2 cups white rice flour
- 2 teaspoons xanthan gum
- 1 tablespoon yeast
- 1 teaspoon baking soda
- 1 teaspoon salt
- 1⅔ cups warm water
- ½ teaspoon vinegar
- 1 tablespoon coconut oil, melted
- Nonstick cooking spray

DIRECTIONS

1. Preheat the oven to 425 degrees. Mix the flour, xanthan gum, yeast, baking soda, and salt. Stir until well blended.

2. Add the water and vinegar, and wait about 5 minutes for the yeast to bubble.

3. Add the melted coconut oil and stir well.

4. Spray a 12-inch round pizza pan with cooking spray. Transfer the dough to the pizza pan. (It will be wet and sticky.) With clean, wet hands, spread out the dough so it fills the pan. Let the dough sit at room temperature for about 15 minutes so it can rise.

5. Ask an adult to place the pizza pan in the oven and bake for 20–25 minutes.

Once the crust is baked, turn to page 75 and follow the directions under "Assemble the Pizza."

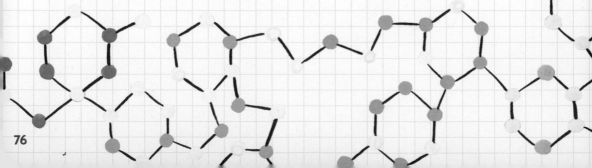

MELBA SANDWICH

 Ask an adult to help you with this recipe.

INGREDIENTS

MAILLARD
REACTION

- 2 slices bread *Try the Overnight Bread on page 72!*
- ½ tablespoon butter
- 3 slices cheese *Try mozzarella or muenster!*
- 4 peach slices (fresh or canned)
- 2 ham slices

DIRECTIONS

1. Spread the butter equally on one side of both slices of bread.

2. With the buttered side facing down, place the bread slices in a cold griddle or frying pan.

3. Place two slices of cheese on the first piece of bread. Then place the peach slices on top of the cheese. Place the ham and remaining cheese slice on the other piece of bread.

4. Carefully flip the second slice of bread onto the first. Ask an adult to turn the burner to medium-low. Cook the sandwich for 3–5 minutes until the cheese starts to melt and the bread turns brown.

5. Ask an adult to use a spatula to turn the sandwich over. Cook the sandwich for another few minutes until the other side is brown.

Ask an adult to check!

RAINBOW CRUNCH SANDWICH

 Ask an adult to help you with this recipe.

INGREDIENTS

- 2 slices bread
- ½ tablespoon butter
- 1 tablespoon hummus
- 2 avocado slices

- 2 slices cheese *Try provolone or havarti!*
- ¼ cup sliced pickled beets
- ¼ cup sweet potato chips

MAILLARD REACTION

DIRECTIONS

1. Spread the butter equally on one side of both slices of bread.

2. With the buttered side facing down, place the bread slices in a cold griddle or frying pan.

3. Spread the hummus on the first slice of bread. Then add the avocado slices and a slice of cheese. Place the pickled beets, another cheese slice, and sweet potato chips on the second slice of bread.

4. Carefully flip the first slice of bread onto the second. Ask an adult to turn the burner to medium-low. Cook the sandwich for 3–5 minutes until the cheese starts to melt and the bread turns brown.

5. Ask an adult to use a spatula to turn the sandwich over. Cook the sandwich for another few minutes until the other side is brown.

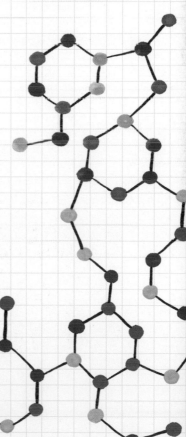

Kitchen Chemistry Lesson

With grilled sandwiches, it's easy to burn the outside before the inside is melted. Understanding the grilling process will reveal the secret to making a melty—but not burned!—sandwich.

When buttered bread is cooked on a heated surface, it turns brown and gets crispy. (The same thing happens to bread cooked in a toaster.) This browning is caused by a series of chemical reactions called the Maillard reaction. During the **Maillard reaction,** amino acids and sugars in the bread react with one another to produce new flavors and textures. (The heat also releases moisture from the bread, helping it turn crispy.)

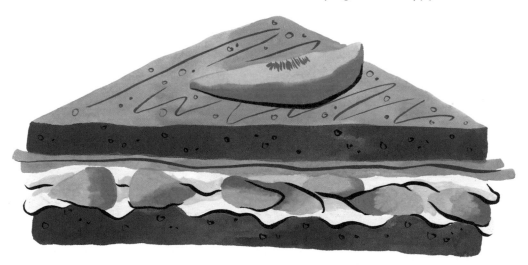

To make a grilled sandwich that's crispy and golden brown, think "low and slow." Keep the burner on a medium-low setting and give the sandwich some time, at least 3–5 minutes, before turning it over and cooking the other side.

CHEWY

CAKEY

CHOCOLATE CHIP COOKIES

CRISPY

GLUTEN FREE

CHEWY
Chocolate Chip Cookies

 Ask an adult to help you with each of the following cookie recipes.

KITCHEN CHEMISTRY LESSON

Shortening has a higher melting point than butter, so it spreads slowly when it's heated. Cookies made with shortening will be softer and thicker.

INGREDIENTS

- 2 cups all-purpose flour
- 1 teaspoon baking soda
- ½ teaspoon salt
- 1 cup shortening
- ¾ cup granulated sugar
- ¾ cup light brown sugar
- 1 teaspoon vanilla extract
- 2 eggs
- 2 cups chocolate chips

LEAVENING MELTING POINT

DIRECTIONS

1. In a mixing bowl, stir together the flour, baking soda, and salt. Set aside.

2. In a separate larger bowl, combine the shortening, sugars, and vanilla extract. Mix until creamy. You may want to ask an adult to use an electric mixer.

3. Add the eggs to the sugar mixture one at a time. Mix well after adding each egg.

4. Add the flour mixture to the sugar mixture a little at a time, stirring after each addition. Stir in the chocolate chips.

5. Shape the dough into balls (about the size of a golf ball), and place them on a cookie sheet covered with parchment paper. Ask an adult to bake the cookies in a 350-degree oven for 10–12 minutes. Let cool.

CRISPY
Chocolate Chip Cookies

INGREDIENTS

- 2 cups all-purpose flour
- ½ teaspoon baking soda
- ½ teaspoon salt
- 1½ cups granulated sugar
- ½ cup light brown sugar
- 1 cup unsalted butter, melted
- 2 eggs
- 1 teaspoon vanilla extract
- 1 cup mini chocolate chips

LEAVENING
MELTING POINT

DIRECTIONS

1. In a mixing bowl, stir together the flour, baking soda, and salt. Set aside.

2. In a separate larger bowl, stir together the sugars and the melted butter. Let sit for 5 minutes.

3. Add the eggs to the sugar mixture one at a time. Mix well after adding each egg. Stir in the vanilla extract.

4. Add the flour mixture to the sugar mixture a little at a time, stirring after each addition. Stir in the mini chocolate chips.

5. Drop rounded tablespoons of dough on a cookie sheet covered with parchment paper. Ask an adult to bake the cookies in a 375-degree oven for 10–12 minutes. Let cool.

KITCHEN CHEMISTRY LESSON

Butter has a lower melting point than shortening, so it'll melt faster and spread more in the oven. Cookies made with butter are flatter and crispier.

CAKEY
Chocolate Chip Cookies

INGREDIENTS

- 3 cups bread flour
- 1 teaspoon baking soda
- ½ teaspoon salt
- 1 cup unsalted butter, softened
- 1 cup light brown sugar
- 1 teaspoon vanilla extract
- 2 eggs
- 2 cups chocolate chips

LEAVENING
MELTING POINT

DIRECTIONS

1. In a small mixing bowl, stir together the flour, baking soda, and salt.

2. In a separate larger bowl, stir together the butter, sugar, and vanilla extract. Mix until creamy. You may want to ask an adult to use an electric mixer.

3. Add the eggs to the sugar mixture one at a time. Mix well after adding each egg.

4. Add the flour mixture to the butter mixture a little at a time, stirring after each addition. Stir in the chocolate chips.

5. Shape the dough into balls (about the size of a golf ball), and place them on a cookie sheet covered with parchment paper. Flatten each dough ball with your hand. Ask an adult to bake the cookies in a 375-degree oven for 8–10 minutes. Let cool.

KITCHEN CHEMISTRY LESSON

Bread flour (the flour used in this recipe) has more protein in it than all-purpose flour. This makes the dough stronger and able to rise higher. More rising gives cookies a cakey texture.

GLUTEN-FREE
Chocolate Chip Cookies

INGREDIENTS

- 2 cups gluten-free flour mix
- 1 teaspoon baking soda
- ½ teaspoon salt
- 1 cup shortening
- ¾ cup granulated sugar
- ¾ cup light brown sugar
- 1 teaspoon vanilla extract
- 2 eggs
- 2 cups chocolate chips

DIRECTIONS

1. In a mixing bowl, stir together the flour mix, baking soda, and salt. Set aside.

2. In a separate larger bowl, combine the shortening, sugars, and vanilla extract. Mix until creamy. You may want to ask an adult to use an electric mixer.

3. Add the eggs to the sugar mixture one at a time. Mix well after adding each egg.

4. Add the flour mixture to the sugar mixture a little at a time, stirring after each addition. Stir in the chocolate chips.

5. Shape the dough into balls (about the size of a golf ball), and place them on a cookie sheet covered with parchment paper. Ask an adult to bake the cookies in a 350-degree oven for 10–12 minutes. Let cool.

LEAVENING
MELTING POINT

KITCHEN CHEMISTRY LESSON

Gluten-free flour mixes can be found at most grocery stores. Usually they're a mix of starches and a gluten-free flour such as rice flour. This mixture of flour and starches gives results that are similar to recipes with gluten.

KITCHEN CHEMISTRY LESSON

CAKE

A cake is a dessert that usually contains flour, sugar, eggs, and baking powder and is baked in the oven. Here are some common cakes and how they're related:

BUTTER CAKE
This cake uses baking soda or baking powder to rise and—you guessed it!—butter as its fat. Most birthday cakes and standard chocolate and vanilla cakes are butter cakes.

Turn the page for a delicious butter cake recipe!

POUND CAKE
This cake gets its name from the ingredients in the recipe. It calls for a pound of butter, a pound of flour, a pound of sugar, and a pound of eggs!

These cakes are all butter cakes.

VANILLA OR YELLOW CAKE

CHOCOLATE CAKE

FLOURLESS CAKE

This type of cake is actually a custard (like a pudding) that's baked, but it looks and tastes like cake.

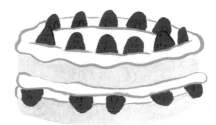

SPONGE CAKE

This cake uses whipped eggs (or egg whites) as its leavening agent instead of baking soda or baking powder.

Chiffon and angel food cakes are sponge cakes.

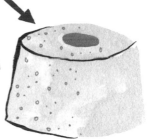

ANGEL FOOD CAKE

This cake is so light and fluffy that it needs to bake in a tube pan; otherwise, it might collapse in the middle. It gets its texture from whipped egg whites and sugar.

CHIFFON CAKE

This cake uses both baking soda and eggs for its leavening agents. And instead of butter, it uses oil.

RED VELVET CAKE

CARROT CAKE

Red velvet and carrot cakes are types of chiffon cakes.

CUPCAKE

This isn't technically a type of cake. It's just a mini cake using a cupcake pan and any recipe you'd like!

VANILLA CAKE

 Ask an adult to help you with this recipe.

INGREDIENTS

LEAVENING
BAKING

- Nonstick cooking spray
- 3 cups cake flour
- 1¾ cups granulated sugar
- 1½ teaspoons baking powder
- ¾ teaspoon salt

- 4 eggs
- ¾ cup butter, melted and cooled
- 1 cup milk
- 1 tablespoon vanilla extract

DIRECTIONS

1. Preheat the oven to 350 degrees. Spray the bottom and sides of two 6-inch round cake pans with cooking spray.

2. In a large mixing bowl, stir together the flour, sugar, baking powder, and salt.

3. Add the eggs, melted butter, milk, and vanilla extract to the dry ingredients. Beat the mixture until smooth, about 1 minute.

Here's how to tell if a cake is done. Ask an adult to remove the cake from the oven. Poke a toothpick into the center of the cake and pull it out. If the toothpick is clean, the cake is done.

4. Ask an adult to pour the cake batter into the greased cake pans. Bake in the preheated oven for 40 minutes or until the cakes are lightly browned.

5. Ask an adult to remove the cakes from the oven, and let them cool in the pans on a wire rack. Let the cakes cool completely before layering and decorating with frosting.

Learn to make this frosting on page 94!

FLOURLESS CHOCOLATE CAKE

✋⭐ **Ask an adult to help you with this recipe.**

INGREDIENTS

LEAVENING
BAKING

- 9 tablespoons butter
- 1 tablespoon plus ½ cup cocoa powder
- 1 cup semisweet chocolate chips
- ¾ cup granulated sugar
- ¼ teaspoon salt
- 1 teaspoon vanilla extract
- 3 eggs

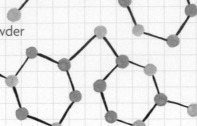

DIRECTIONS

1. Preheat the oven to 375 degrees. Grease the bottom and sides of a 9-inch springform pan with 1 tablespoon of butter. Sprinkle 1 tablespoon of cocoa powder in the pan. Shake the pan over a sink to coat the bottom and sides with the powder.

2. Place the chocolate chips and the remaining butter in a microwave-safe mixing bowl. Microwave on high for 30 seconds. Stir the mixture; then heat for another 30 seconds. Keep stirring and heating for 30 seconds until the chocolate and butter are melted.

3. Add the sugar, salt, and vanilla to the chocolate mixture and mix well. Add the eggs, stirring until smooth. Add the ½ cup cocoa powder and stir until just blended.

4. Pour the batter into the prepared pan. Ask an adult to bake the cake for 20–25 minutes. When it's done, the top will have a thin, hard crust.

5. Ask an adult to remove the cake from the oven and allow it to cool for 30 minutes. Then remove the cake from the pan, and allow it to cool completely. Right before serving, sprinkle a little powdered sugar over the top of the cake.

Buttercream Frosting

INGREDIENTS

- 1 cup unsalted butter, softened
- 4 cups powdered sugar
- 2 teaspoons vanilla extract
- pinch of salt
- 2–4 tablespoons milk

DIRECTIONS

1. Place the butter in a mixing bowl. Use a spoon to beat the butter until it's creamy.

2. Add the powdered sugar, vanilla extract, and salt to the butter. Beat the mixture until it's light and fluffy, about 2 minutes.

3. Add 2 tablespoons of milk and stir until well mixed. If the frosting is too stiff and difficult to spread, add another 1–2 tablespoons of milk and mix again.

EMULSIONS

Other Flavors

CHOCOLATE

Follow the instructions for Buttercream Frosting but add ½ cup cocoa powder in Step 2.

STRAWBERRY

Make the Strawberry Sauce on page 44. Chill the sauce in the refrigerator. Follow the instructions for Buttercream Frosting and add the sauce to the mixture in Step 2.

If the frosting gets too soft, beat in another 1–2 tablespoons of powdered sugar.

Kitchen Chemistry Lesson

Frosting is another emulsion—similar to butter and whipped cream. When you blend frosting ingredients together, you whip air into the mixture. The air bubbles are held in place by the fat molecules in the butter and milk.

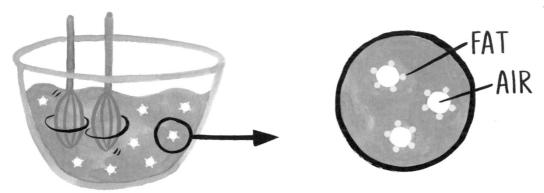

FAT

AIR

Frosting Fun

Here are some ways to decorate cupcakes with frosting:

DIP

Heat 1 cup of frosting in the microwave for 15 seconds. Stir the frosting. It should be runny. Turn an unfrosted cupcake upside down and dip the top into the frosting. Give it a slight twist and lift the cupcake up. Set the cupcake right side up to set.

SWIRL

Scoop ½ cup of frosting into a plastic sandwich bag. Press the frosting into one corner and twist the bag so the frosting doesn't leak out the top. Use scissors to snip off the corner of the bag. Starting in the center of an unfrosted cupcake, gently squeeze the bag and swirl the frosting around in a spiral.

WAVE

Use a butter knife to dab some frosting on the top of the cupcake. Keep adding dabs of frosting until the cupcake is covered with a thick layer. Then use the knife to draw waves in the frosting.

CHOCOLATE BARK

 Ask an adult to help you with this recipe.

INGREDIENTS

- 1¼ cups milk chocolate chips
- ½ cup assorted mix-ins

DIRECTIONS

1. Cover a baking sheet with wax paper. Make sure your hands, bowl, and utensils are completely dry.

2. Pour the chocolate chips into a mixing bowl that's microwave-safe. Ask an adult to microwave the chocolate for 30 seconds at a time until it's melted. Stir the chocolate with a spoon until it's smooth.

3. Ask an adult to pour the candy mixture onto the wax paper. Use a spoon to spread the mixture evenly.

4. Sprinkle the mix-ins over the melted chocolate.

5. Let the bark cool completely. Then break it into 2-inch pieces. Store in an airtight container.

MELTING POINT

Here are some mix-in ideas: dried fruit, pretzels, almonds, peanuts, cereal, granola, or candy sprinkles!

Kitchen Chemistry Lesson

CHOCOLATE

Chocolate is usually a mixture of cacao powder, cocoa butter, and sugar.

Cacao beans (also known as cocoa beans) are the seeds from the cacao tree. Cacao trees are a type of evergreen tree that grows large seedpods. They're native to South America. Cacao seeds are ground into a paste before they're used to make chocolate.

Plain cacao beans taste bitter like coffee beans.

Cocoa butter is a vegetable fat that comes from the cacao bean.

Most chocolate is made up of these ratios:

CACAO 10%–20% | MILK SOLIDS 8%–16% | SUGAR 32%–60% | COCOA BUTTER 10%–20%

The melting point of most chocolate is 93° F.

CHOCOLATE MELTING TIPS

• Chocolate is very sensitive to temperature and must be melted slowly.

• Chocolate and water don't mix! Make sure all your utensils and bowls are dry before melting chocolate. When chocolate melts, the dry and liquid ingredients are broken up. If water is added to melted chocolate (even a few drops!), the dry ingredients are attracted to the water and they clump together. This is called *seizing*, and seized chocolate will look grainy and lumpy.

Cooking Up History

Today we know a lot about food: how it works to fuel our bodies, how to grow it, how to cook and prepare it, and how to keep it safe for eating. Here are some people from history who helped us better understand and enjoy the food we eat.

Nicolas Appert
(1749–1841)
Chef Nicolas Appert spent 14 years trying to develop a new way to preserve food. When he succeeded in 1810, the French goverment paid him to make his invention public. Appert's method involved filling jars with food such as soup or vegetables, sealing them, and then boiling the jars in water. His method was called *appertisation,* but today we know it as canning.

Malinda Russell
(1812–1866)
Cook and pastry chef Malinda Russell ran a successful boarding house and pastry shop before publishing *Domestic Cook Book.* It was the first cookbook published by a person of color in the United States. Drawing on her experience as a pastry chef, Russell's book was filled with recipes for fancy desserts such as rose cake and a French specialty called *floating island.*

Amelia Simmons
Very little is known about Amelia Simmons, who lived in the newly formed United States after the Revolutionary War. One thing we do know: She wrote the first American cookbook! It was called *American Cookery,* and it was published in 1796. Simmons likely didn't have a formal education and lived in the Hudson Valley area of New York.

Louis Pasteur
(1822–1895)
Scientist and inventor Louis Pasteur discovered another new way to preserve food. In 1864, he invented a process that killed bacteria in milk and other foods by heating the food and then cooling it very quickly. We know this process today as *pasteurization.* Pasteurization helps foods last longer and kills harmful bacteria that can make people sick.

Fannie Merritt Farmer
(1857–1915)
After she had a stroke as a teenager, Fannie Merritt Farmer spent time at home learning to cook. Later she enrolled in the Boston Cooking School and eventually went on to become the school's principal. In 1896, she published *The Boston Cooking-School Cook Book*, the first cookbook to use standardized measurements (such as cups and table-spoons) and the first to explain the chemistry involved in cooking!

Prudencio and Carolina Unanue
When Prudencio and Carolina Unanue immigrated to the U.S. from Spain and Puerto Rico, it was difficult for them to find familiar foods in their new country. They started an import business, introducing Spanish and Latin American foods to a larger audience. Today it's the largest Hispanic-owned business in the United States.

Julia Child
(1912–2004)
Famed cookbook author and TV chef Julia Child didn't know how to cook until she was in her thirties. But after studying at Le Cordon Bleu (a famous French cooking school), she coauthored her first cookbook. Through her books and TV shows, Child taught American audiences to cook French cuisine in their own kitchens.

Edna Lewis
(1916–2006)
In 1948, when there were few women chefs, Edna Lewis worked at her first restaurant in Manhattan. Her special-ties were inspired by the food she grew up eating and cooking in Virginia. She went on to become a bestselling cookbook author, award-winning chef, and ambassador for traditional Southern cooking.

Joyce Chen
(1917–1994)
Shortly after immigrat-ing to the United States from China with her family, Joyce Chen opened a restaurant specializing in northern Chinese cuisine. At her restaurant she introduced the idea of an all-you-can-eat buffet so customers could try different foods. Later Chen wrote cookbooks, starred in a cooking show on TV, and developed a line of food products including stir-fry sauces and cooking equipment.

FOOD SCIENTIST
DR. MAYA M. WARREN

Tell us about what you do!

I'm a food scientist (and senior director of research and development) who specializes in the science of ice cream and other frozen aerated desserts. Some call me Dr. Ice Cream!

How did you become a food scientist?

When I was six years old, my parents gave me an ice cream maker! I loved it and wanted to learn more about what I was actually doing to make the liquid inside turn into ice cream. I fell in love with chemistry in high school and majored in chemistry in college. I wanted to apply this science in a more applicable way, so I decided to become an expert in all things ice cream!

How would you describe your typical day?

I spend much of my time working with product development teams in other countries like Taiwan, Kenya, Egypt, and Pakistan. I have conference calls first thing in the morning, and then I'll spend time making new flavors of ice cream in my company's lab. In one day I may make and/or taste more than 30 flavors of ice cream, sorbet, or frozen yogurt!

What's your favorite part of your job?

I love everything about my job! Who wouldn't want to eat ice cream and travel the world?!

What's your advice for kids who want to do what you do?

There are many different routes one could take to become a food scientist, but it is important to study classes in STEM (science, technology, engineering, and math).

FAVORITE ICE CREAM FLAVOR: Sweet cream

PEOPLE I LOOK UP TO: My parents

PHOTOGRAPHER & STYLIST
SUNSHINE FRANTZ

Tell us about what you do!
I'm a food and product photographer. The work I do is what some people call "styled photography," which means I arrange ingredients, props, and dishes in a scene so that everything looks nice together.

How did you get started as a photographer and stylist?
I've loved taking photos since I was a kid, but I didn't think I'd want it to be my job because I thought professional photographers had to take photos of people, and I preferred still-life photography. For many years I was a graphic designer. Over time, I realized I loved styling scenes and taking photos even more than graphic design!

Where do you find inspiration?
I'm always inspired by nature. I have a big garden, and I'll go out there and look at the way the light hits the leaves or think about the colors I'm seeing.

What's your advice for kids who want to try styled photography?
Try this: Whenever you put food on a plate, think about how to make it as beautiful as you can. Think about the colors and shapes and how they look together. I like the saying "we eat with our eyes first," which means if the food is beautiful to look at, we will enjoy the experience of eating it more!

What's your favorite food to photograph?
Salads are fun because there are so many textures, colors, and layers to play with!

I ONCE WANTED TO BE:
A marine biologist

SALTY OR SWEET:
Both!

FAVORITE PROP:
Linen tea towels

BAKERY OWNER
ANNEMARIE MAITRI

Tell us about what you do!
I own two bake shops: one big, one small. I have a passion for baking from scratch, sourcing local ingredients, and creating delicious, memorable experiences for people.

What's your favorite part of your job?
Baking. Honestly, there isn't much I don't like about my job. But getting in the kitchen and creating? Yep, that's hands-down my favorite part.

Did you have any education or training before becoming a bakery owner?
I am self-trained in baking. In terms of business management and human resources, I have an undergraduate degree and a master's degree.

Describe your typical day.
Most days begin at four a.m. and can easily wrap up well after dusk. Being an entrepreneur means there is no typical day. Some days I bake all day. Some days I coach decorators and bakers on my team. Some days I quietly answer e-mails, settle up on accounts, and dream up new recipes or menus.

What's your proudest moment on the job?
Realizing that I can make a choice to create and grow a business that makes conscious decisions to impact my community and the environment in positive ways.

What's your work uniform?
A T-shirt, jeans, vintage apron, and a dusting of powdered sugar!

FAVORITE DESSERT:
A warm cookie

FAVORITE SUBJECT IN SCHOOL:
Reading

I ONCE WANTED TO BE:
An astronaut

ORGANIC FARMER
LAUREN RUDERSDORF

Tell us about what you do!
I'm an organic CSA vegetable farmer. My husband, Kyle, and I own and operate a farm that grows organic vegetables for a CSA and several restaurants in our area.

How did you become a farmer?
I grew up on a farm but never thought I wanted that life. Later I learned about organic farming and community-supported agriculture, where the farmers have a real relationship to the people who purchase and eat their food. After college, my husband and I decided that a CSA farm was a perfect fit for our skills and passions. My husband had a college degree in soil science, and I was exceptional at shaping a business.

How would you describe your typical day?
Every month of the year looks a little different. In winter we're planning like mad and making important purchases. In spring, we're seeding in our greenhouse and getting the first crops into the ground. Summer involves a lot of planting and a lot of harvesting, selling, and fieldwork. Fall means the work is waning, but the harvests are still heavy and abundant.

What's your favorite food to grow?
I love to grow everything in the onion family: garlic, scallions, shallots, onions, leeks. I love the way they grow, keeping them weeded, and the beautiful layers and complex flavors.

A community-supported agriculture (CSA) farm sells produce directly to people who purchase a membership. Members often receive a box of produce every week or a couple of times per month directly from the farm.

Cookbook Author
Andrea Debbink

Tell us about what you do!
I write and edit books for American Girl, including this one! I wrote *Kitchen Chemistry*, plus I developed and tested all the recipes in the book.

Did you have any education or training before writing a cookbook?
I studied journalism and history in college, but I don't have any special training in cooking. I've loved to cook since I was a kid! Most of my knowledge comes from reading about cooking and food science. Then I practice my skills by trying recipes and learning from my mistakes.

What's your advice for kids who want to do what you do?
Know that you don't have to be an adult before you can learn to cook, study food science, or create recipes. You can start right now! Also, know that it's okay when recipes don't turn out the way you expect. When I was creating recipes for this cookbook, I made a lot of mistakes: banana bread that tasted bitter, gluey oatmeal, and burned cookies. Making mistakes is how you learn, especially when it comes to cooking!

What's your favorite thing to cook?
I love baking cookies and different types of bread. My favorite things to bake, however, are scones. The recipe I use has dried cherries and chocolate chips.

What's your work uniform?
When I'm testing recipes in the kitchen, I always wear clothes I can get dirty, including an apron. I'm a messy cook!

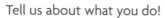

PEOPLE I LOOK UP TO:
My grandparents

I ONCE WANTED TO BE:
An Arctic explorer

FAVORITE RECIPE IN THIS BOOK:
Banana bread

CHEF & RESTAURATEUR
ANN KIM

FAVORITE FOODS: Pizza and tacos

PEOPLE I LOOK UP TO: My mom and dad

FAVORITE ITEM ON MY MENU: Roasted cauliflower

Tell us about what you do!
I'm a chef and owner of three restaurants.

How did you become a chef and entrepreneur?
My love of cooking and creativity inspired me to become a chef. I also wanted to be in control of the decisions that were made in our business, so I chose to be an owner. My work doesn't feel like work, because I believe in what I do and I always try to have fun!

Tell us about your restaurants.
Pizzeria Lola was named after my dog, Lola. Hello Pizza was inspired by the idea of being friendly and welcoming. Young Joni is named after my mother, Young, and my husband's mother, Joni. Our mothers inspire us to be our best selves, so we decided to name the restaurant after them!

What's your favorite part of your job?
Collaborating with my chefs at each restaurant on new and delicious dishes for our menus. I also love eating pizza every day!

What's the most creative recipe you've invented?
Korean BBQ pizza. I wasn't sure if people would like this mix of flavors, but it's our number-one selling pizza.

What's your advice for kids who want to do what you do?
If you love cooking, make time to cook and get better at your craft. Ask questions, stay curious, be open to possibilities, and be fearless.

Kitchen Chemistry Dictionary

Here are the definitions of some science-related words that appear throughout the book.

acid: a chemical substance recognized by its sour taste

aroma: scent or smell

carbohydrate: a nutrient that gives the body energy

carbon dioxide: a colorless, odorless gas that naturally occurs in the air

cellulose: a type of fiber that makes up the cell walls of plants

chemical: anything that is made up of matter. Here are some things that are not made up of matter and therefore are not chemicals: energy, sound, gravity, and heat!

chemical reaction: a process in which chemicals are combined and change into one or more new chemicals

coagulation: the process of changing from a liquid to a thickened mass

emulsion: a mixture of two substances that wouldn't normally mix

evaporation: the process of turning liquid to vapor

fats: substances that help the body store energy and help process some nutrients

fiber: a carbohydrate that the human body can't process; it helps move other foods along in the digestive system

food allergy: when a person's immune system mistakes what is typically a harmless ingredient for something harmful that it needs to fight

food intolerance: when a person has trouble digesting a certain food or ingredient

freezing point: the temperature at which a liquid changes to a solid

gluten: a mixture of proteins that are found in most grains such as wheat, barley, and rye

leavening agent/leavener: a substance that introduces air into dough or batter, helping it to expand and rise

maceration: the process of softening something by soaking it in a liquid

Maillard reaction: a chemical reaction in which heat causes acids and sugars to make food brown and crispy

matter: any substance that has mass and takes up space

melting point: the temperature at which a food changes from a solid to a liquid

molecule: the smallest physical unit of an element

nutrient: a substance that provides nourishment for growth

pectin: a starch, a type of carbohydrate that exists naturally in fruit

protein: a nutrient that supplies energy and builds muscles. It also helps give food its structure and texture.

receptors: special types of cells or nerves that take in information and send it to the brain

viscosity: the stickiness or thickness of a substance

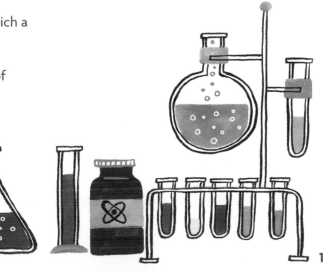

Did you enjoy this cookbook?

Write to us!
Kitchen Chemistry Editor
American Girl
8400 Fairway Place
Middleton, WI 53562

Here are some other American Girl books you might like:

Each sold separately. Find more books online at americangirl.com.

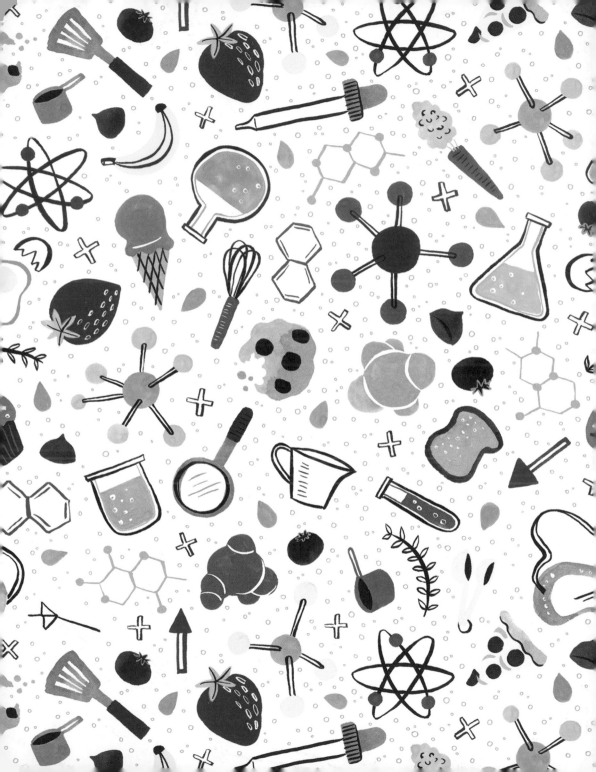